THE JOURNEY TO THE UNKNOWN

THE JOURNEY
TO THE UNKNOWN

by

TZE-SI HUANG

FONS VITAE

First published in 2014 by
Fons Vitae
49 Mockingbird Valley Drive
Louisville, KY 40207
http://www.fonsvitae.com
Email: fonsvitaeky@aol.com

Copyright Fons Vitae 2014

ISBN 978-1891785-70-2

Printed in China

Library of Congress Cataloging-in-Publication Data

Huang, Tze-si, 1938-
   The journey to the unknown / by Tze-si Huang.
      pages cm
   Summary: "Autobiography of a Chinese national who immigrated to the United States after World War 2, living first in Taiwan and then in New York City; profusely illustrated with drawings"—Provided by publisher.
   ISBN 978-1-891785-70-2
   1. Huang, Tze-si, 1938-2. Chinese Americans—Biography. 3.   Immigrants—United States—Biography. 4. Chongqing (China)—Biography. 5. Taiwan—Biography. 6. New York (N.Y.)—Biography. I. Title.
   E184.C5H859 2014
   973'.004951--dc23
                        2014023183

Contents

There is a man who makes a meal of golden clouds:
where he dwells the crowds don't go.
Any season's just fine with him,
the summer just like the fall.
In a dark ravine small droplets fall, keeping time,
and up in the pines the wind's always sighing.
Sit *there* in meditation, half a day,
a hundred autumns' grief will drop away.

Han Shan
Chinese Ch'an Buddhist poet
Tang Dynasty

BIRTH

I was the tenth child born in the family, and I was born after my mother carried me for twelve months. It was a strange phenomenon. I was always sick in my early years. Later I learned that my father had consulted a well known fortune teller about my fate right after I was born. It was foretold that the child could not grow up and that he might not survive beyond the age of ten. There was a small chance that the child could survive if he renounced the family and was adopted by a person who did not have offspring. Sometime later I was adopted by a Buddhist nun as my mother.

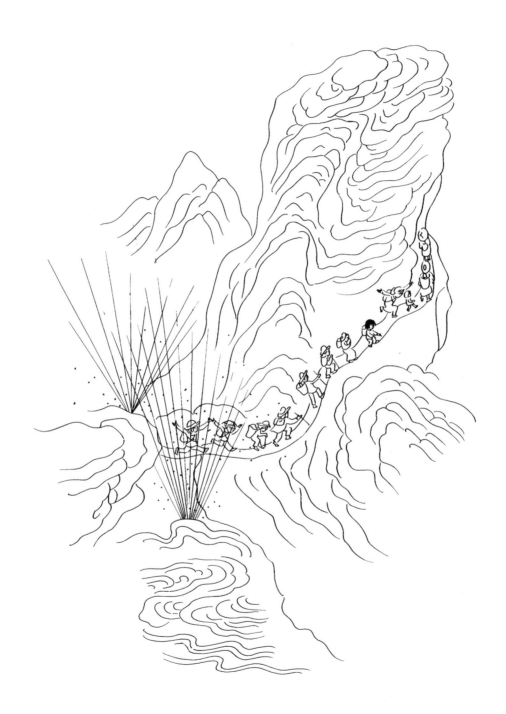

SCHOOLING

I never attended kindergarten. I started primary school at about age five, which was interrupted by the Japanese invasion and civil wars. I was constantly on the move as a refugee.

About a year later I passed the entrance examination permitting me to attend the 4th grade in a different town. After one semester, I moved again to another town. Where I attended school for two years. That was the end of my schooling.

BOMBING

During the war, the city of Chungching, the war capital, was bombed day and night by the invading Japanese. It was considered the most bombed city in the world. Every day and night, wave after wave of Japanese bombers dropped bombs indiscriminately, killing thousands and thousands of civilians. After each bombing, I saw human parts hanging on trees all over the place. Several times the bombs hit so close, I was thrown up several feet in the air and was covered with mud and human blood. It was horrific.

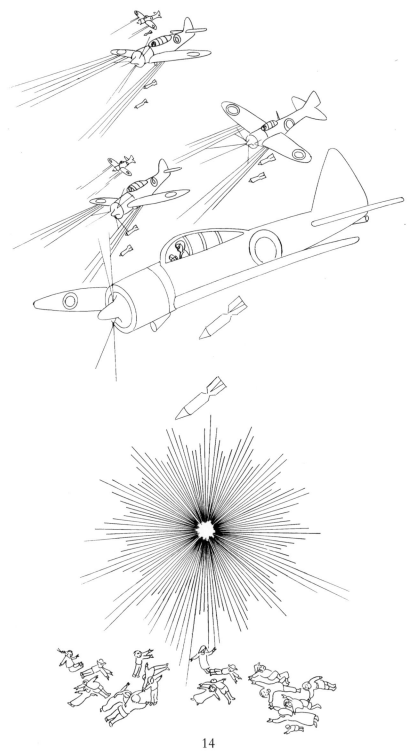

Many times the Japanese fighters flew very low and massacred civilians with machine guns. My mother's brother (my uncle) and four of my brothers and sisters were all killed. The city was burning, day and night. Life was so fragile, so transient. Each day could be the last day; each moment could be the last moment.

DEPARTURE

After the Japanese surrendered, Civil War broke out. Again I moved, moved endlessly.

Finally, a new government was established.

Then, under some special circumstance, of which I understood nothing, I said good-by to my family and to my adopted mother, and then started at the age of nine years old!

On one very early morning, my elder brother, carrying a lantern, took me to the boat station. I was sick and vomiting the whole way. I boarded a junk, carrying a small suitcase with a blanket and a few summer clothes inside. My mother gave me a small gold ring and a few silver dollars. Later I lost the ring, unfortunately.

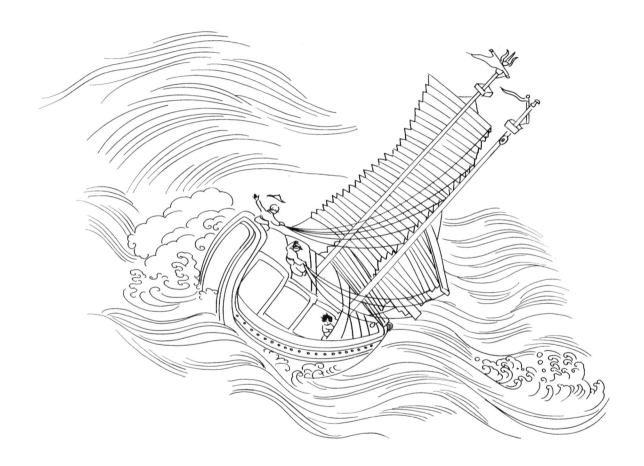

THE JOURNEY

The Yangtze River was treacherous, so the journey was dangerous. When the boat arrived at Wuhan, known as one of the three furnace cities in China, it was horrendously hot. I, and many others camped in a big empty building. I was very sick with a high fever, and vomited continuously even without taking food. With a high fever in the hot summer, in the hottest city of China, I felt as though I were in an oven wracked with great pain.

It was unbearable.

After some days, the heat and pain inside me started receding. I was very weak, and it seemed that I was slowly leaving my body. I struggled to open my eyes, but to no avail. Finally, I left my body and started flying. While I was in the air, I looked down at my body, and the image of my mother's sad face appeared. So, I struggled to come back to my body. A few days later, my fever completely disappeared, and I resumed my journey by junk towards the Unknown.

I arrived in Shanghai and after stowing away on a steamship, landed in Hong Kong. From there, I travelled by ship to Taiwan.

TAIWAN

During the journey from Hong Kong to Taiwan, I was seasick and had no food for the entire trip. The ship arrived at the southern port city of Kou-shion. I was hungry and exhausted. I bought a bowl of noodle soup but was sick again right after I ate it. At the dock, there were many gangs who pressured me to join them. Miraculously I escaped, and found a Buddhist Temple where I rested for a while in the care of a few monks.

The monks advised me to travel north to the Chinese refugee camp. I saw a train, destined for the city of Taipei, the provincial capital, where most civil war refugees were living. I thought I might have a better chance to survive there. I boarded the train, which had open cars with military men and weapons. It was very cold when the train started. I was trembling. A military man took off his jacket and gave it to me along with two wheat buns. I am forever grateful for his kindness. Without that jacket, I could not possibly have survived the coming winters. The train stopped in many places. At long last I arrived at a small town about 15 miles from the city of Taipei.

I found some odd jobs in a military factory. But I did not make even enough money to eat. I often stole ears of corn from the farmer's fields. One time, while I was stealing corn, several dogs chased me. I ran away quickly but fell on a rock, breaking my right arm about two inches above the wrist. A piece of bone stuck out. Immediately I pushed the bone back into place. It was extremely painful. But the fear of becoming disabled was far greater. At that age, I did not have the knowledge that the bone could reconnect. Of course, I could not have any medical treatment.

I gathered pieces of canvas and made a small tent by a bamboo grove, a few hundred feet from a hanging bridge over a river. It was very cold in the winter and very hot in the summer. Rainy days were miserable. When the current of cold wind blew down from Siberia, I put everything I owned on top of me, and still it was too cold to sleep. This affected me deeply. Since that time, I have always had a problem sleeping.

SOME EVENTS

English

I would get some odd jobs in the day, working in a factory, but spent most evenings in the local library. I read whatever books I could get. Once I came across "Lincoln's Biography." It was bilingual, one side was in English, the other side in Chinese translation. I tried to match the two languages. That was the beginning of my learning English. I never studied English in school.

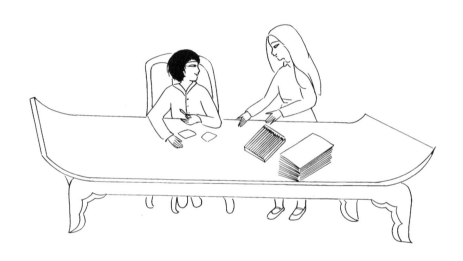

Pencils and Paper

I liked drawing. The paper I used was scrap paper. In the library, where I went to sketch, there was a very well dressed and good looking girl about my age. Her father was a high official. Whenever she came to the library, she was always followed by several well dressed older and stronger boys.

One evening, this lovely girl came over to me and said, "You are very economical. Scrap paper is not very good for drawing and writing. And your pencil has only two or three inches left." Then, she offered me a box of pencils and a stack of wonderful paper. From then on, she always sat next to me in the library.

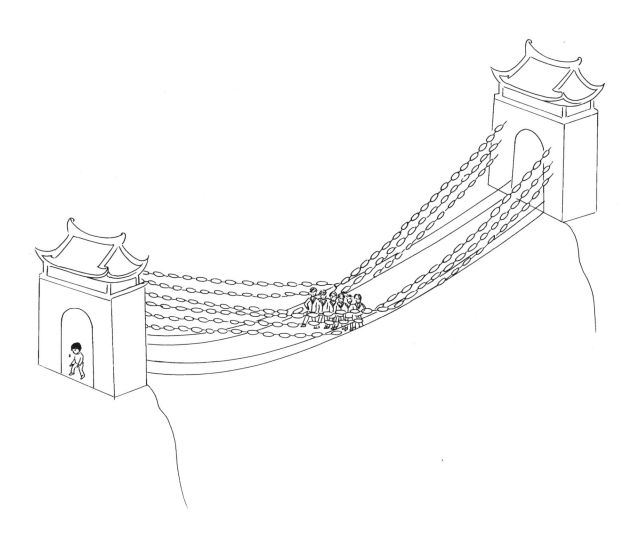

Life Threatened

About a week later, one evening when I went "home" from the library I came across the same well dressed, older and stronger boys blocking my way in the middle of the hanging bridge. They threatened me, demanding I stay away from that girl. Otherwise, they said that they would kill me on the spot and throw me into the river. I was small and alone. What could I do? I complied. When I got home, I cried bitterly and was very ashamed of myself for giving in to their demand. I could not forgive myself.

Attacked

One day, I was watching people play basketball and was talking with a new friend, a young girl about my age. Suddenly, someone threw the basketball at my chest from a few feet away with full force. It hit me so hard that I fell on the ground and almost suffocated. My chest so painful that I could not get up again until the girl helped me. A while later, I felt a salty taste inside my mouth. It was blood.

The girl was the youngest of four daughters from a very respectable family in the town. Many young men were anxious to know them. I supposed the young man who hit me with the ball most likely could not bear to see this girl had made friends with a small, lowly laborer. From then on, every day after work when I walked by her house she always watched me from her balcony. We never got together again. Many years later, I was told that the man who had hit me in the chest with the basketball had died of lung cancer.

Fly with the Wind

Life was hopeless. I was constantly in a state of despair. I loved music, and often sang my heart out when I was alone. When a huge typhoon came, I often went to the middle of the hanging bridge at night. The bridge was swaying, the wind was howling, and the river was roaring in the darkness. Oh, let this torrential rain wash away my sorrows! How much I wished that I could fly with the wind and disappear from the world!

During the autumn, I often went to the forest, and sat by the stream. I watched leaves falling from trees into the stream, flowing and flowing until they disappeared into the unknown.

How similar this was to my own life!

Sounds From the Chirping Birds

One day, I suffered a severe abdominal pain, along with a high fever, vomiting and diarrhea, most likely due to food poisoning. It lasted several days. Slowly, slowly, the fever receded and the pain subsided.

I was very weak, lying alone in my tent. It was so quiet and peaceful, except for a few sounds from the chirping birds in the bamboo grove. I thought that it would be a wonderful way to leave this world. Alas, I still had a vain hope of seeing my family and my adopted mother again— sometime in the unknown future, even though the chances were very remote, indeed. I still remembered my adopted mother, and our cooking red rice and vegetables together at the corner of a small old Buddhist temple years before. In those days, communication between China mainland and the island was prohibited. Violation of this was a serious matter subject to severe punishment.

TO THE CITY

City of Taipei

The situation was so hopeless that it finally became unbearable.

I was the fifteen years old. I decided, no matter what the risk would be, that I must leave the factory.

Nobody that worked there ever left, because there was virtually no opportunities for anybody without connections and/or a college degree. I had barely entered primary school and had not even finished it, and I did not have any connections, but I left the factory anyway. I found some odd jobs in the City of Taipei, and made barely enough to buy the cheapest food, but I did not have enough left for renting a place I would stay.

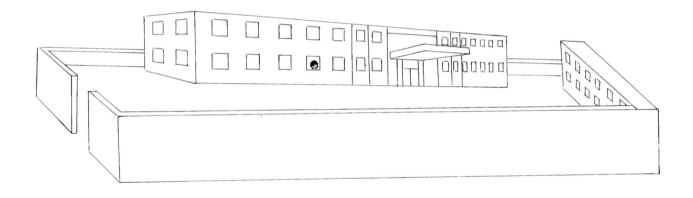

TB Dormitory

One day, I met a university student who said that I could stay with him in the student dormitory which was exclusively for students with tuberculosis. No other students dared come near it. I knew what the danger would be for a teenager like myself living in such an environment, but I moved in anyway because I did not have any choice. I could not set up my tent in the city zoning. I was constantly haunted by the fear of possibly being infected with TB, and that I might die soon after. I stayed in the Tuberculosis Dormitory for about a year, and blessedly the TB virus spared me.

Attacked

I often frequented the University Library where I met a girl. She lent me her textbooks.

We became very good friends. One evening when I was walking in the University campus, several individuals surrounded me. They demanded that I stay away from that girl because their leader was interested in her. Suddenly they attacked me. I was badly beaten. To this day I still have a big scar on my right arm.

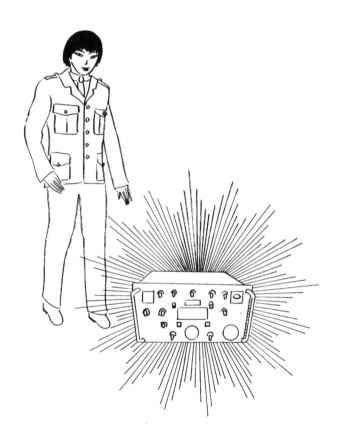

Army

I joined the Army where food and board was provided along with a small monthly salary, which was enough to buy a few extras. At first I was assigned to monitor the military activities in the Taiwan Strait.

At that time, the two sides of the Strait between China mainland and the island were still at war. Later the Commander picked me to assist him in coordinating with the American advisors. I was still a very, very young teenager. This appointment caused lots of jealousies and hostilities among the staff of the commander. I left the Army after two years.

The Army had many radios. I would listen to the B.B.C. as much as I could, to try to get better in English. One day I got "the invisible key" to the language, and that was the rest of my English schooling.

University

Again, I was wandering in humanity, existing marginally. One of my friends from the University was very helpful to me. He knew I was anxious about going to school, as I did not have any documents to prove qualification.

As he was very creative, he forged a certificate for me so that I was able to register for the entrance examination which was conducted by the Ministry of Education annually. It was very competitive. Unexpectedly, I passed the examination and became a university student. But I worked several jobs much of the time. I taught in English School and did translation work. For this reason, I missed many classes. I often fell asleep in class.

One day I was called by the Chairman of The Economic Department to his office. He inquired why I missed so many classes and often fell asleep in class. I told him that I had to work day and night in order to pay tuition and living expenses. In addition, I had to support my family on the mainland. He was very sympathetic.

In those days China was very poor. Reports of starvation were constantly in the news. I often skipped one meal a day in order to save some money and send it to a family friend (whom I never met) in Hong Kong. He would then convert it into Chinese currency and send it to my family.

I did not know where my family lived, nor their condition, as all communication was still prohibited.

Time went by fast. At the university, just before my first final examination, I was again called by the Chairman of the Economic Department to his office.

He showed me a document from the Ministry of Education. It read, "The student Tze-si Huang has committed document forgery. Therefore he should be expelled from the University." I was stunned and felt very ashamed. I could not face the Chairman. But the Chairman was very kind and sympathetic. He said, "You are an excellent student. We don't want to lose you. You can appeal to the Ministry of Education and continue to study here." I appealed three times and all three appeals were rejected. The situation was hopeless.

The Minister of Education

Pressures came from all directions. I could not sleep. I tried everything, including a specific request to the officials handling my case. All my efforts failed. I was completely exhausted and in total despair. In my desperation, I decided to appeal to the Minister of Education, himself, directly.

Of course, the chance of seeing the Minister was almost impossible. I prepared an appeal and went to the ministry. The Minister's Assistant told me that the Minister could not see me.

At that moment, an idea dawned on me, that the Minister's last name was the same as mine: Huang. Then I said, "My name is Huang. It is a family matter." Then he let me into the Minister's office. I submitted my appeal to him, and gave a brief presentation. The Minister called in the Chief Legal Consul of the Ministry.

The Consul said, "This student has appealed three times and all three have been disapproved." He added, "This student should have been expelled from the University." The Minister said, "Though this student has come into the university through a side door, he has proven himself qualified. We should find some way to help him." He sent the consul away. After some deliberation, he wrote the following words on my appeal: "Due to bad behavior of the student, two major demerits are recorded. Status of Matriculation is approved." That was the end of that long struggle.

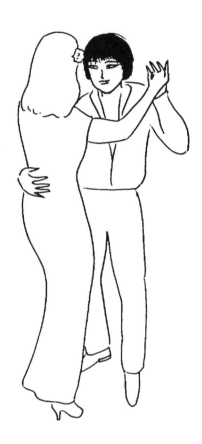

Graduation

At last I became a formal student at the very end of having been already almost four years in the University. For years, I had been longing but unable to go to school as other people did, because I didn't have money or any record of my schooling. Now my matriculation had been approved, and graduation was approaching. I should have been very happy.

Instead, I was depressed. Graduation became an anticlimax. I did not even attend the graduation ceremony.

In those days, on the island of Taiwan, there lived basically two groups of people: the native Chinese and the recent new-comers following the retreat of the National Government. They were government officials, educators, civil servants, business communities, academics, educators, teachers, scientists, military people and their families. They had their own spaces and styles.

I lived in the very narrow gray area as an outcast, struggling to survive.

Graduation brought many opportunities, but it also brought me a deep feeling of emptiness. I declined several very good offers. I pondered the meaning of life. Trying to fill the emptiness, night after night, I spent my life in nightclubs, and danced my life away. But it only deepened my feeling of emptiness. I found the nightclub life completely meaningless and a waste of life.

Buddhism

The seed of Buddhism, which was inside me since I was little with my adopted mother, started to sprout. I turned to the teaching of the Buddha. I often walked hours to visit Buddhist temples deep in the mountains. Sometimes I stayed there for days.

The Buddhist gong in the misty dawn, the drum in the dusky evening, the discipline, the quietude, the meditation all gave me a new found solace and meaning of life. I began to think of joining the order and spending the rest of my life in the mountains. However, how could I withdraw my support for my family? I was the only son left who could help.

SIGNIFICANT DEVELOPMENTS

Some formative university experiences were the following, from the time I attended the University until my departure for the United States:

Being Cheated

In my sophomore year, I secured a major translation project from English to Chinese. I worked day and night for several months in the hot summer, in a tiny room. The project brought me a good amount of money, enough for me to live a simple life for one semester, including tuition. I planned to take it easy for the semester. One night, a schoolmate came to me asking for help. He said that his mother was in a very critical condition and required immediate surgery to save her life. He said he did not have money to pay the hospital. In those days, hospitals in Taiwan did not accept patients without paying first, regardless of the condition of the patient. Since it was urgent concerning life and death, I lent him almost the whole amount of money just received from my hard work.

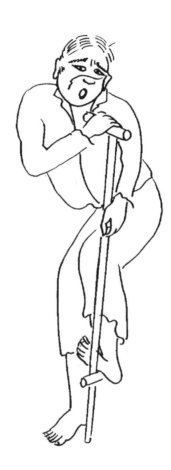

Later on I found out that there was no surgery. I was cheated. I lost all the money. About a year later, I ran into him, hobbling down the street. There was a huge scar in his swollen face. His front teeth were all gone. Clearly, I was not the only one he had cheated.

Although he caused me great pain, I spared him but others did not.

Special Committee

One day, I was called to the Office of the Chairman of the Economics Department. The Chairman showed me a document from the Special Committee under the Premier of the Government, requesting all universities in Taiwan to recommend their best student graduates to participate in a special test.

The purpose was to choose the best talents to work for a newly created organization to develop ways and means for further economic development for the island. The Chairman told me that he intended to recommend me to the committee for the test. I said that according to the requirements of the document I was not qualified. First, I was only in my junior year, and second, I did not consider myself among the best students. But he said, "You are special. I'll make a special recommendation to the Committee for you so that you can participate in the test."

There were more than 100 participants for the test. I thought to myself that it was impossible for me to compete with them. In addition, I did not think that I did well in the test. Hence, I forgot the whole thing right after the test because I did not think I had any chance. About a month later, unexpectedly, I received a letter from the Special Committee that I passed the test and an interview had been scheduled for me.

I did not have any decent clothes to wear for the interview. A friend lent me a sports jacket which did not fit me very well. The interview was intense and intimidating. The interview team was composed of seven officials from high level government, including several Cabinet members. To my great surprise, I was chosen one of the top three in the area of economics. I was immediately hired for the organization. The work was very demanding. It paid very well. Within a year, I was recruited to be on the staff of a Special Financial Committee, headed by the Minister of Banking and Currency. He also served as a member of the Special Committee. The function of the Financial Committee was to review all Taiwanese financial and banking policies and practices, and to make recommendations for necessary changes in order to promote economic development.

The Golden Cage

On one occasion, the Minister said to me, "I can see that you possess many qualities to be successful. However, it would be a great help if you had a wealthy and powerful family behind you. I have talked to a friend of such a family about you. They have an only daughter about your age, a gentle and good looking girl. You'll like her. I'd like to introduce you to the family. They are anxious to know you. I hope that I can be the match-maker for you."

This put me in a very difficult position. How could I say "No" to the good will of such an important person for such a great opportunity? However, I did not want to get married. Particularly not to the only daughter of a wealthy family. By accepting the offer I might gain a great deal. But also, I might lose my independence and dignity. A bird inside the cage is a prisoner, even if the cage is made of gold. I wanted to fly. With great difficulty I declined the proposal.

The Secretary General

In the beginning of my senior year, a new professor came to the class. He said that he wanted to know the students better and asked that each student write a composition on the subject of one's own choice. So we did. He singled out my composition as superior. After that, he invited me to his home many times. One day, he told me that the Secretary General of the President had been looking for young talents to be groomed for future leaders. He said that he had observed me closely for many months and wanted to recommend me to the Secretary General. He would like to arrange an interview with the Secretary General for me.

In those days, many people with much better qualifications than mine would be honored to have such an opportunity. The interview with the Secretary General appeared to go well. I was informed that the Secretary General intended to appoint me to his staff as the first phase of my training. In addition, the Secretary General would have a plan for my future development. After careful deliberation I declined the opportunity.

It was a very difficult decision, indeed. On the one hand, if I accepted the offer, my commitment would be total. I would devote my whole life to serve the country and at the same time fulfill the Secretary General's expectation of me. On the other hand, I was not sure whether I would fit into the constricted life of a government official.

U.S. F.B.I. Far-Eastern Operation

A little earlier, I also had been recruited by the F.B.I. Far East Operation with a very attractive financial offer. At that time I was very poor and barely surviving. However, I declined the offer because I could not bring myself to spy on the country of my birth. In addition I did not think that I could live happily as an F.B.I. agent.

Comic Relief

Although I did not accept the offer by the Secretary General, a letter from him triggered a comical experience. At that time, I was working as a reporter for World News Reporting.

Usually I came home about 2:00 A.M. every night. I lived in a tiny room on the top floor of a two-story house. Downstairs lived a family with three daughters. One of them came to see me pretty often. It appeared that she was interested in me. Her mother did not want her daughter to have any relationship with such a poor student like me.

And so she began banging on the walls, and making loud noises when I was sleeping in hopes that I would quickly leave the unbearable house. We shared the front door of the house and inside, there was a separate stairway to my room. Once, when I came home, to my great surprise, both mother and daughter greeted me with broad smiles. I wondered what had happened?

They both invited me into the living room and served me tea. The daughter had dressed up and was posing like Marilyn Monroe. It was quite amusing. Then they handed me a letter from the Secretary General, which had been hand delivered by a messenger from the Presidential Palace. From then on there was no more noise, but lots of smiles. Visits from the daughter became more frequent. I was alarmed, as I never had any desire of developing a relationship with her. I realized I must get out of that situation as soon as possible. I secretly rented a tiny room far away from the house. One day when the family was not home, I took my simple luggage and moved out of the house altogether.

Encounter with a Prostitute

One night I was walking home from work about 1:30 in the early morning. It was very cold. At the corner of a narrow street, a very young prostitute approached me. I told her that I was not interested. She said that if she could not make some money she would be beaten up by her boss.

I told her that I would give her the money, but I did not want her business. She said that she could not take the money without the actual business, because her boss would still beat her up later. So she begged me to go with her as a cover, pretending that the business did happen. I went with her to a tiny room. She showed me some scars on her body. She was very thin and sickly. I gave her the money and sat there for about 15 minutes, then left. I was deeply affected by this experience. I was not able to sleep that night. I was sorry for those girls and angry at society. I thought that it would be better for a soldier to die a quick heroic death in the battle field, than for that girl and many other girls in similar situations, who had to suffer a slow and agonizing death.

The Full Moon Festival

Mid-autumn festival is one of the three most celebrated festivals in China. On one full-moon festival night, I walked through a street full of activities even after midnight. On that special occasion many people had stayed late to enjoy and celebrate the festival. I saw a middle-aged man, well dressed, lying on a pedicab, calling "Mother, Mother!" on and on. He was old enough to be my father. It was a strange scene to me, indeed. I suppose that mother is the source of life. Whenever one encounters difficulty, one turns to that source for help and comfort; when one achieves success one tends to attribute it to that source. No matter how old one is, in an unguarded moment of innocence, one always remembers the mother. Mother and child are connected in the heart. Any other kind of love might eventually fade away. Only the love from the mother lasts forever. On the other hand, all people grow old, but not all people grow up.

Teaching

As usual, I worked more than one job at the same time. One day I walked by an English training school. Out of curiosity I went into the school and met the owner/principal. He told me that there were many university graduates who applied for visas to study in the United States, and that they must pass an English test given by the U.S. Consulate.

The purpose of his school was to help those people for the test. He inquired whether I was interested in registering in his school. We started to discuss the program and I made some suggestions. Then he invited me to join the teaching faculty. In my first class, the students looked at me with disbelief. I was so young (I had not finished my college yet), and I had long hair down to my shoulders.

In those days I did not have enough money for the barbershop. I always cut my own hair, but on that day I had not found time to do so. Sensing the student's misgivings I said that the goal of this program was not for regular English study. The focus was to prepare them for the test given by the Consulate. The most difficult part of the test was writing composition. "You'll be given about 20 minutes to write a composition." I said that I had designed ten topics. I believed these ten topics would cover any topic given in the test. I added, "We'll practice together. You pay for the practice but I receive payment for the practice. If anybody has any reservations, it is not too late to withdraw from this class." Nobody withdrew.

Appointments by the School of Journalism
and by the University

It went very well. I conducted the program very differently from other teachers. Most of my "students" passed the test. I became very popular. I conducted many classes and made good money.

About the same time, a senior co-worker from the newspaper informed me that the College of Journalism had an instructor position open. There were several senior news reporters who applied for the position. He recommended me to the President of the College. After an interview with the College President I received a letter of appointment the next day by special mail.

Upon my graduation, I received a letter of appointment as Teaching Assistant from the university. I went to see the Chairman of the Economics Department to inquire about the appointment. He said to me, "During the past four years you have worked terribly hard but did not have time to study. Now this is a good opportunity for you to make it up through teaching."

I thanked him profusely for his kind consideration. But I told him I was anxious to leave Taiwan, and to go and see the world. Therefore, I would not be able to accept his kind offer and asked for his forgiveness.

Guest of Honor of the Chinese Government

In my senior year, an important leader of the Chinese Community in San Francisco was invited by the National Government to visit Taiwan. At that time, the National Government was very shaky and isolated after being defeated in the mainland.

Great efforts were made to secure support from overseas Chinese, particularly those in the United States. Against that background, that gentleman was invited by the government with great honor. He only spoke his native tongue. Nobody in the press corps understood him fully. I happened to understand him better. As such, I was invited to accompany him in his many activities. Before his departure, he invited me to dinner.

He told me that he was very happy during his trip and that he had met many important people, including the President. Now he was leaving. He'd like to offer me a great opportunity. He'd like to sponsor me to go to the United States to work for his Chinese newspaper. In the spare time, I could go to school.

I thanked him but declined his offer because I did not want to owe anybody anything. In addition, I was uncomfortable with his patronizing attitude. Inside of me, I had decided that if I wanted to go to the U.S., I'd go through my own effort. In those days, people on the island were very worried about their futures.

They feared that someday the mainland would take over the island and everybody would suffer. Therefore, many people tried every possible way to get out of Taiwan and go anywhere else in the world. Of course, the U.S. was always the first priority. People considered the U.S. as paradise.

Passport and Visa Process

The road to leave the island was not smooth. For many years, I had been recruited by the political establishment on various occasions, in various ways, including promises of benefits, coercion, and even threats. I always refused to comply.

As a result, I was considered politically incorrect, meaning I was on a black list. Hence, my application for a passport was stalled unless I obtained a guarantee from two high officials. The next obstacle was the visa to the U.S. At that time, the U.S. Consulate had two unwritten rules: visas would not be issued to applicants without family and property.

I went to the U.S. Consulate without much confidence of getting the visa since I did not have a family or any property. The meeting with the Consul turned out to be a pleasant surprise. We had an interesting conversation on literature. Then he said, "We welcome you to the U.S."

Departure from the Island

Now everything was in place. I was ready to leave the place where I had spent my formative years. There had been sweat and tears; hope and despair; successes and failures; joy and sorrow. For the one who loved me I had to say goodbye, sadly. I did not want to have a family.

I did not tell anyone of my departure date. Quietly I went to the airport alone, and departed. When in the sky, I gave a last look at the island thinking that I may never see this place again.

NEW YORK CITY

J.F.K. Airport

After a long flight the aircraft landed at Kennedy International Airport, New York City on a Sunday morning in January, about 8:00 A.M. I went out to get a cab, but failed. There were no people, no cars. It was as if the whole place was deserted. The sky was gray, almost dark, gloomy and heavy. It was very, very cold.

Graduate Student

Finally a lady with a British accent helped me get a cab to the city. I checked into a small hotel, a few blocks away from Central Park.

A few days later I registered in the Graduate School of New York University as a foreign student. During classes, the heat put me to sleep since I had never been in a place with heat. I squeezed my legs as hard as possible to keep myself awake.

New York City Seaport

One evening, I took a walk in Battery Park, at the tip of Manhattan, alone. There were no people around, only piles of snow. When the last ray of evening light gradually disappeared, the sea and the sky became one. A thin layer of smoke covered the whole seaport.

Looking at a ship moving out of the port slowly into the darkness, suddenly my vision was blurred. I found that my cheeks were covered with tears. Oh! Life!

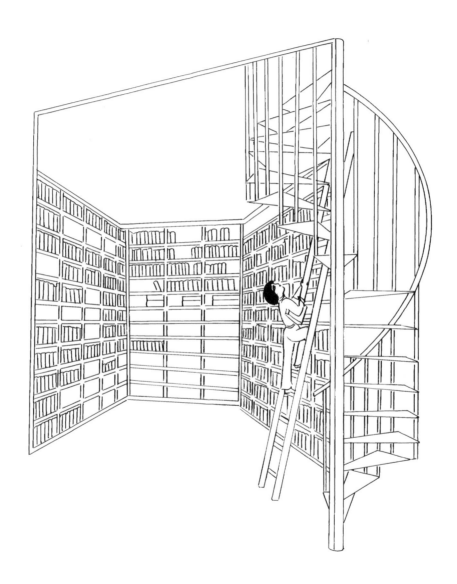

School Library

I got a part time job in the school library system. Besides me, there were several students who worked in the same section. All of them spent most of the time reading and doing homework. They rarely worked. Most of the time I was the only one who worked. One day there was a time gap and I studied a little. The librarian called me to his office and said, "You are fired." I asked him, "Why?"

He said, "You cannot read books during work hours. You China man." I was so angry I said, "All my co-workers read books and do homework during work hours. Why do you pick on me? I'll report this case to the Student Association."

Then I picked up the phone on his desk and dialed The Student Association. He tried to stop me, but I stared at him and told him sternly, "Don't ever touch me!" That was my first experience with discrimination in the U.S. After that I've encountered all kinds of discrimination, some brutal, some subtle.

Summer Resort

Summer came. I got a job as a waiter in a summer resort in upstate New York. It was a strange experience for me to serve people in a restaurant and to receive tips. It took some time for me to get used to it. One lady guest invited me to dance. Then she said, "I don't want you to eat the hotel left-over's. I'll order the best dishes for you, and you'll have them in my room with me." But I sensed what was in her mind and I declined her invitation.

Another lady guest, about 40, invited me to take a ride in her car. Then she drove to a lake, surrounded by a forest, which was very quiet and without a soul.

I sensed what was in her mind, too, and was alarmed. Quickly I jumped into the lake and swam across at full speed. It was at least 500 feet. I took a rest on the other side for a while.

By the time I swam back, it was time for me to go back to work. So I avoided any further activities with her. I received frequent invitations from the lady guests. It was difficult to reject their invitations without being offensive. At the same time I did not want to get involved with them. In addition, it caused a great deal of jealousy with my co-workers. So I quit the job after a few weeks.

Death of a Friend

In the same summer resort I ran into a gentleman whom I had met as a teenager. At that time in Taiwan, he had already completed his masters degree and was a faculty member in a university. But now he worked as a waiter in restaurants. After I returned to New York City, he visited me frequently and confided to me that he was fired by the resort and had been fired from many other jobs as a restaurant waiter. He was not able to keep any job. He said that nobody understood him or were willing to listen to his plight. He kept on asking me why people were so cruel and why they treated him so badly?

I suggested to him that when he worked as a waiter, he must conduct himself as a waiter, not as a scholar.

One evening when I took the subway home, people were talking about a Chinese man who had jumped from the 36th floor of Rockefeller Center and had killed himself. Immediately I knew that man must be my friend. A couple of days before he had borrowed some money from me and said that he wanted to have some enjoyment.

Taiwan Agent

During my first year in the U.S. I was approached by a Chinese who wanted to be friends. I was open to that. He visited me frequently in the beginning. But before long he started following me wherever I went, and then began accusing me of being a Communist. He claimed that he knew everything about me and stated that he saw me conducting a meeting with a group of Communists. Of course, all his claims were completely untrue, but I could not get rid of him.

At the same time I got several phone calls every night, from late night to early morning. When I tried to answer them—all was silent. So I was not able to sleep. It was very disturbing.

F.B.I. "Interview"

Clearly, this was the work of The Taiwan Intelligence Operatus.

One day I received a document from the F.B.I. for an "interview." It was a surprise. What could I do?

I mentioned this to three lady friends. They all volunteered to go with me to the interview. They suggested it was dangerous for me to go alone.

During the "interview," three agents questioned me repeatedly in various ways for more than three hours about the following things: are you a Communist and how many American girls have you slept with? It was most annoying.

At the end, they could not find any proof that I was a Communist. Then, I asked them why I had to be questioned? They showed me one document addressed to the F.B.I. accusing me of being a Communist. The large folder of documents that they could not show me. Clearly, it was the work of The Taiwan Intelligence Operatus. The purpose was to get me deported back to Taiwan. If that happened, the consequence would really be very serious.

After the "interview" my friends in the waiting room told me that they were thinking about going to The New York Times if I did not come down for another two hours.

Experiencing Discrimination

One afternoon at about 5:00 P.M., I was walking from Madison Avenue and 44th Street towards the New York City Public Library at 42nd Street. Suddenly, a tall man pointed his finger at me and cursed, "You f------ China man. Go back to where you came from!" Then, without warning, he attacked me. Quickly many people gathered around, watching. Nobody intervened. I saw a policeman nearby. He just looked but did not stop the attack.

One winter evening, I was forced at gunpoint to lie down with my face in the snow. At another time, a young man rode his bicycle towards me at full speed. I was hit and thrown on the ground several feet away. The man looked at me and laughed. There were many other episodes.

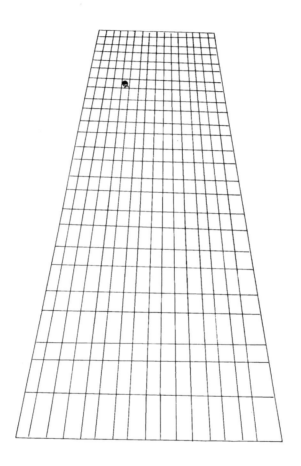

U.S. Corporate Life

At the completion of my second semester, I started looking for a regular job. Within one week I got three offers from three Fortune 500 Companies. I was advised by the employment agency to take the offer from one particular company. So I accepted the offer as an Assistant Manager in the Chemical Division.

One morning about three months later, my boss told me that a representative from the headquarters would come that afternoon to make an important announcement. He asked me to inform everybody about it. A gentleman came from the headquarters that afternoon. He announced that the Chemical Division had been sold. All personnel in the Division would be laid off. People were stunned. After a moment of silence, some ladies started sobbing. Some people said that they had devoted 20 or 30 years of their lives to work for the company and counted on the company for their retirement. Now they were thrown away like old shoes. It was my first time witnessing the brutal reality of U.S. corporate life.

The next day, I got a phone call from The Director of Human Services of the headquarters. He said that he was very sorry for what had happened. He added that since he was the one who convinced me to join the company I would receive three month's severance pay. At the same time, he had found a comparable position in another division for me. I accepted the offer and joined the other division. My new boss was very tedious and talked endlessly. It was very unpleasant. A few months later I quit and joined another Fortune 500 Company, working directly under the C.E.O., along with three co-workers.

We were extremely busy. Almost every day we worked from 9:00 A.M. to 10:00 P.M.—sometimes even Saturdays. One of my colleagues called his wife every day from the office. From his tone I sensed that there was a trace of apology and uneasiness. How could one be a good husband or father when one worked such long, exhausting hours? Each week an Executive Bulletin was circulated among the people with executive positions. I considered it a gimmick.

From time to time, we had lunch with the C.E.O. Whenever he told a "joke," we laughed dutifully regardless of whether it was laughable or not. It was such a burden on me. I was exhausted all the time. Except for working, there was no time for myself. About a year later I had enough and quit. I swore to myself that I'd never work for any U.S. Corporation again. I never did.

A Free Bird

Now I was a free bird. But I still needed to make money to live. I tried my luck in the travel business. I got into the Charter Flight business. In those days, a round trip charter flight from New York City to London cost half the price of a regular flight. Hence, charter flights were very popular, particularly for students who wanted to travel in Europe. London airport was the major connecting center.

Many Jewish students in the New York City University system went to Jerusalem through London. I recruited several of them from the university and offered them half of the profit when they brought clients to take the flight. I made good money from that business. Every time I went to the bank to make a deposit, the manager immediately came over and filled out the deposit slip and made the deposit for me. I did not have to wait in line. Money talks!

The Match-making Trip

Most Chinese students that came to the U.S. to study from Taiwan in the 1970s and 1980s had to study and work at the same time. Life was extremely busy and difficult. The students had very little social life and were very lonely. As they were also getting older, having a family became an urgent matter. But there was very little opportunity for them to meet each other.

The head of the Taiwan Student Association consulted with me as to how to help students to meet one another. Since I was in the travel business, I suggested we conduct a two-day trip to Toronto, Canada. I believed that the trip might provide opportunities for participants to meet each other, if we did it right.

About 100 people participated in the trip. I arranged for two big busses, and assigned one male and one female as co-captains in each bus. Their responsibilities were to maintain order and focus on creating opportunities for participants to meet one another. I told them that this was a match-making trip.

During the journey, a young lady constantly talked to me, and tried to sit close beside me. My only purpose was for the student's match-making, not my own. I did not want to get involved with anybody.

As soon as we checked in to the hotel in the City of Toronto, I quickly went to Chinatown for supper. While I was waiting for my food, the same young lady came in and asked to share my table. I could not politely refuse. But when the food came, I quickly finished it and left. During the remaining time of the trip, she still made every attempt to talk with me.

I was very careful about expenses. I wanted to save as much money as possible so that I could give it back to the participants. Though whatever was saved should have become my business profit, I considered the trip as my mission. At the end of the trip I divided all the savings with the participants. They were very happy and surprised. They thanked me profusely.

The next day I got a phone call from that ardent young lady accusing me of corruption.

Of course, it was completely untrue. I just listened to her and did not respond to her charges. I told her that she could talk as long as she wanted to. It was clear to me that by falsely accusing me, she was hoping I'd respond and explain. When I said nothing, she suddenly pretended to make up an apology and invited me to a lunch or dinner of my choice so she could see me again. I did not fall into her trap.

The Bardo Ceremony

I learned that my father had passed away. Hoping to comfort his soul, I made a special trip to the city of Taipei where there was a Buddhist temple, which offered Bardo Services for the deceased. I arranged a special Bardo Ceremony in the temple for him in the very big hall. Several ceremonies were taking place at the same time. Everyone of them had a big photograph of the deceased with the dates of birth and death erected on a big wooden board. Everyone of them had a group of monks and many family members participating in the ceremony. There were gongs and drums and bells and lots of noise, and when the services ended, all of them left.

I was left alone with one monk.

I did not know my father's dates of birth or death, nor did I have his photograph. I just wrote down his name on a piece of paper.

At the end of the ceremony, I burned incense and paper money, and made other special offerings at the back of the hall. I looked at the smoke that rose and circulated in the quiet hall and then vanished into the sky. I was overcome by waves of profound sadness; a chill penetrated my whole body in the middle of that very hot summer day. I did not know where I was.

With a heavy heart I departed the next day.

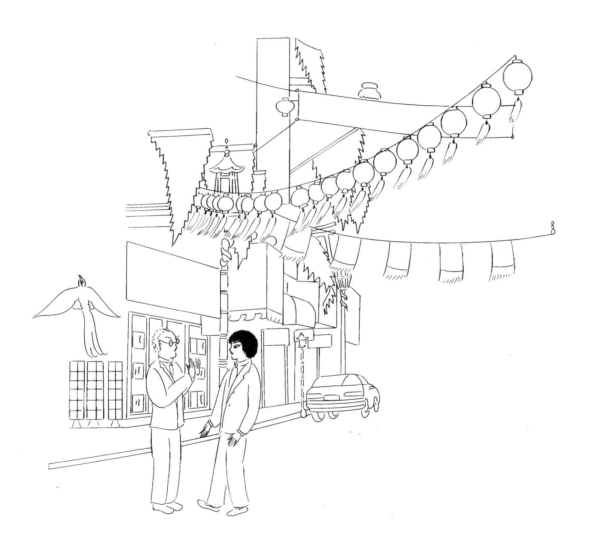

My Brother in San Francisco.

I knew I had an elder brother who left China many years before. I had no idea where he went. I remembered vaguely that he carried me on his shoulders, when I was little, down to the river to swim. Through my continual quest to find my family, I discovered that he was in San Francisco, and owned a stationary/bookstore in Chinatown. I made a special trip to San Francisco to see him.

When I went to the bookstore I asked a very pleasant man there about my brother. He asked me who I was and why I wanted to see him.

I told him that I was his brother. Suddenly, the man's tone changed completely. He said, "There is no such person here."

Judging from his tone and expression, I was very sure my brother was there. But I didn't know why he wouldn't want to see me.

Exclusive Elite Club

On a certain occasion I met a young lady from Taiwan. She was extremely friendly to me. She called me every day and frequently invited me to dinner. Finally, she proposed marriage. I did not respond to her proposal. Trying to induce me into the relationship, she told me that she was a member of an exclusive elite club (which was not known to the public.) Membership in the club was very restrictive. Only the offspring of the most powerful and famous families from the Imperial time downwards could be admitted and had to be recommended by two current members. She had secured two members to recommend me for the membership. She said that, as a member, I would benefit in many ways so as to advance my future.

She also showed me the membership list of less than 200 people. I recognized that all of them were indeed very wealthy and influential. I told her I did not want to be part of any club. I wanted to live my own way.

Health Systems Consultant

A New York University classmate's family had strong connections with the high authorities of New York City, and got me a consulting position in the Health Systems Agency of the City. At the time, I knew nothing about the health care system.

My first assignment was to review an application submitted by a Maternity Center in the mid-town East side of Manhattan. The first thing was to do an on-site evaluation and meet the applicant. Two lady co-workers were assigned to assist and coach me. During the meeting, one of the ladies took over the whole process. Since it was my project, what she did was rather inappropriate. The next day, my boss invited me to his office. He told me he had learned that one of the ladies had dominated the meeting and asked me how I felt about it. I told him that she was a mother. A mother has natural concerns about maternal matters. I said I was grateful for the ladies' active participation. Then he said, "You are very gracious. You'll go far."

A few months later, the lady who had dominated my first project ran into trouble and asked me for advice. She also suggested that she introduce me to a beautiful girl from the Mensa Club of which she was a member. But I wanted to decline her kind offer.

Later on, I was assigned to the Manhattan Borough division of the Agency responsible for project review. The director of the division was a 6' 7" African American man. He was very abusive to all the staff. All the staff members asked me to stay in the office as much as I could, for whenever I was not there, they suffered the director's abuse.

One afternoon, I was discussing something with the director in his office. He told me curtly, "You call him and tell him that I want such and such things!"

I was irritated by his attitude but more so by his abusive treatment of all the staff. I decided to give him a lesson. Even though I am only 5' 5", I threw his phone on the floor and yelled at him, "Make the call yourself! I am not your secretary!" Then I stormed back into my office. He followed me. I yelled at him, "Get out of my office! Don't ever come in here again without my permission!" He said, "You don't respect me." I said, "You are damn right!"

The next day the Deputy Director from the headquarters called me and said, "I heard what happened yesterday. You are OK. Don't worry about him."

Manhattan was a very complicated place. It had the richest and the poorest. We divided the Borough into several districts. I had to go to many meetings in all districts, dealing with all kinds of people. Many meetings took place in the evenings.

One evening, I attended a meeting in the middle of Harlem. On the way back a man with a bottle of liquor in his hand quickly approached me. It looked dangerous. To diffuse the situation I grasped his bottle and said loudly, "Give me a drink!" He stared at me and then hugged me and then said, "You are my brother! You are my brother!"

Why not? We are all brothers and sisters. We all come from the same source to which we'll return. Our appearances may be different, but our essential nature is the same. We are one.

Assistant Director

I had worked for the Agency for almost two years. Then I got a phone call from the Executive Director of a Health Systems Agency in upstate New York that covered 7 counties. He said that he had heard about me and that there was a position in his agency. He wanted to discuss this with me, and I told him that I did not drive and could not meet him there. He offered to come into the city to meet me.

We had lunch in the Hilton Hotel, NYC. This gentleman came with his wife. He immediately offered me a position of Assistant Director. I declined because it was inconvenient for me to go there. But in the evening of that same day, he called me at home and said, "I'll give you a promotion, and I'll get somebody to drive you to work until you can get your driver's license." I could not say "No" to him.

A few days later, my Deputy Director of the Agency invited me to his office in the headquarters. He told the secretary that he would not answer any phone calls during his meeting with me. When the door was closed, we had a long discussion. He asked me not to leave the Agency. He said, "Within two years I'll make sure you'll be in one of the top positions. I can facilitate this as I will soon take over the position of Executive Director. I told him that I had already accepted my offer and could not withdraw from my commitment. Finally he said, "I'll always reserve a place for you. All you need to do is call." I never did.

My first assignment in the new agency was to establish a long-range plan, which would consolidate all maternity facilities of 49 hospitals in the seven-county region. It was a very complex, highly political, emotional and controversial project. In one of the many public hearings, one man close to the podium where I sat shouted loudly, "That f------ Chinese comes here to close our hospitals! God damn him!" Right after the hearing I went directly to him and said, "Sir, I know that you are concerned about the project. I'd like to invite you to my office. There we can discuss it more fully."

Business Proposal

My office was about 15 minutes away from one of the richest towns in the United States. It had a quiet, very respectable Italian restaurant. I had lunch there every day. One day the owner invited me to dinner. He said that he wanted to discuss a business project with me. During dinner, he told me that the residents of this town were among the richest in the U.S. He wanted to convert the restaurant into a Chinese Palace style building, and open a first-class Chinese restaurant.

In order to attract rich customers, a person with class must be present. He said I was that person. He proposed that he'd provide all the resources for the conversion and the operation. I would be in charge of the operation of the proposed restaurant. Ownership would be 50% 50%.

It was a great proposal. I consulted many people in the restaurant business.

It was concluded that the project was workable. It was quite tempting. After careful deliberation, I declined, regrettably because I did not want to be tied down long hours every day in a restaurant.

Deputy Director

A year later, the Executive Director wanted to return to the West Coast and resigned. The new Executive Director and I did not get along well.

Just at the time I was thinking of resigning I got a phone call from a friend of mine, a professor in the NYC New School. He informed me that a Health Systems Agency was looking for a Deputy Director. He wanted to recommend that I meet the Executive Director of that Agency. During the luncheon interview with the Executive Director, I was offered the position of Deputy Director. She even said, "I want you to know that we are equal partners." I was most touched and grateful for her trust.

In the first staff meeting, I announced that I'd like to know everyone better, and asked the secretary to arrange a personal meeting for each staff member. I emphasized that it be arranged by alphabetical order, not by rank, so everybody was Number One.

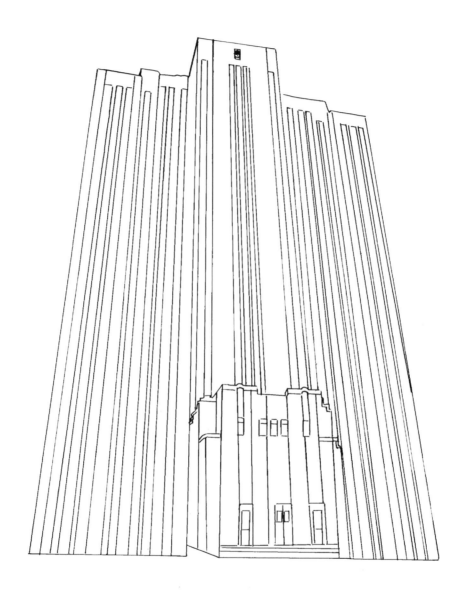

Executive Director

Before I joined the Agency, a report from the U.S. Congress Review Team had brought up a long list of issues to be corrected. My first task was to address and correct those issues.

Working closely together with the Executive Director, we reorganized the Agency, reassigned work and made many changes. Within three months, we had corrected all the issues brought up by the Review Team.

About a year later, my boss resigned from the Agency and took a job as the President of the New York Mercantile Exchange, one of the four major exchanges in the United States. The Agency was undertaking the task of searching for a new Executive Director. The search committee received more than 300 applications.

I selected three of the most qualified candidates for the Committee and the board of Directors to consider. However, they would not consider any of the applicants, insisting that they would appoint me to be the Executive Director. Officially, the Board of Directors must vote for the appointment. During the Board meeting, I declined to attend because I did not want my presence to affect the vote. However, inside of me I had already decided that I couldn't accept the appointment if there were even one negative vote or abstention. Shortly after, they invited me back to the Board meeting and showed me that the result was unanimous. I accepted the appointment of Executive Director, and thanked the Board for their trust.

TSE-SI HUANG

Executive Director

As Executive Director of the Agency, one of my aims was to create the best environment in which members of the staff could function to the best of their capacities. I had many responsibilities. I had to work and deal with people from all segments of society, such as: labor unions, racial groups, political, religious and various professional groups, as well as civil groups, too. In addition, I had to work with the Federal, State, and local governments.

I also attended many meetings of different natures. Besides this, I was invited to teach Health Care Economics at the Jersey Campus of the State University, and serve on its advisory committee.

Washington D.C. Conference

My first time, in the capacity as Executive Director, attending a National Conference in Washington, D.C., I had some interesting experiences. At the reception desk, a young lady took out my name tag. My name and that of the organization were there, but my title was not.

She asked, "What is your title?" I said, "Would you please check the registration form?" Then she found my title in the form and said, "Really?" I laughed as she typed my title on the name tag.

When I put on my name tag, immediately I encountered some subtle and not so subtle hostility towards me in the Conference Hall.

During lunch, all the attendees had assigned seats. At my table, there were three other men. They completely ignored me. They passed things back and forth right in front of my face, and did many other things trying to make me as uncomfortable as possible. However, I sat there comfortably,and enjoyed my lunch regardless of their hostile activities. At that time, I felt like I was the only person existing in the entire world.

The next morning, while I was having breakfast alone in the dining room, I was also reading a Chinese book. I noticed that several men were watching me. After some time, one of them came over and asked to share the table. I said, "O.K.," but I did not pay him any attention.

After a while he asked, "What is the language in the book you are reading?" I said, "Chinese."

"What kind of book?" he asked. "Sutra". I said. "What is sutra?" he asked. "A sutra is the teaching of Buddha. He spent more than 40 years teaching how to find self-realization."

"Buddha is not as good as Jesus," he said. "Jesus is greater than Buddha." I replied, "I respect Jesus as much as I respect Buddha. They both have made a great contribution to human spiritual development. Buddha emphasized compassion versus the universal, unconditional love of Jesus. However, love is a happening.

You cannot control it. Love is like a flower that opens in your heart. It emits fragrance. When you don't have such universal unconditioned love as you claim you have, you are a Christian in name only. Your so-called love is only a plastic flower without any fragrance."

★

Defending Charges

Every month I had to explain and defend my decisions on various health care projects in the State Health Care Coordinating Council. One afternoon, the Director of Project Review came back from the Review Committee of the State Health Care Council, pale and defeated. He reported that one of the applicants for a major project I had disapproved, had sent an eight-page letter to all members of the State House and the Governor's Office, without our knowing, and accused my decision as biased. It was a serious charge.

Based on the copy of the letter, I dictated the response. In the full Council meeting I requested to address the charges made by the applicant. They brought in a large group of people who shouted, "Out of order!" I insisted to the Chairman that it was absolutely essential that the charges by the applicant be addressed fully before any decision was to be made by the Council.

Finally, I was able to respond to the charges. And as a result, my decision was unanimously upheld.

Authority versus Responsibility and Leadership

After the meeting, the lawyer who had prepared the letter of charge came over to apologize to me. Similarly other battles were fought from time to time. These gave me lots of insight as to how to operate within the U.S. society.

One time, a reporter asked me, "Based on the Federal and State laws and regulations, can you tell us what authority you have?" I said, "I don't have any authority. I only have responsibilities. I try my best to carry out my responsibilities responsibly, and hope to earn the trust of the people whom I serve."

Another time at the conclusion of a three-year review by the Congress Review Team, some member commented that the agency staff represented the agency and me very well. Someone asked me how I considered my leadership style and whether a leader could be trained.

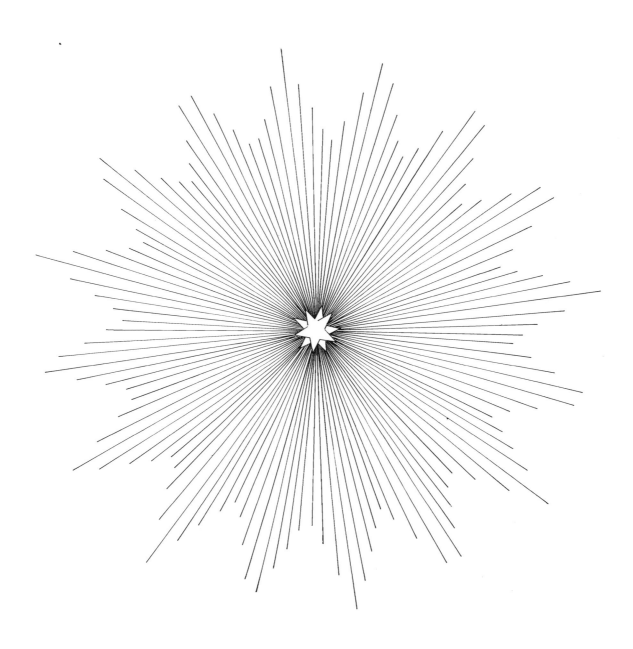

I told them that I believed respect, consideration, understanding, and encouragement were essential. I did not believe in coercion or rule by fear. I believed the highest form of leadership was effortless. For when you are genuinely accepted and respected, the wheel turns by itself without anyone's doing.

I did not think a leader could be trained. A piece of stone no matter how much you polish it remains a stone. A piece of diamond, even a raw one, shines.

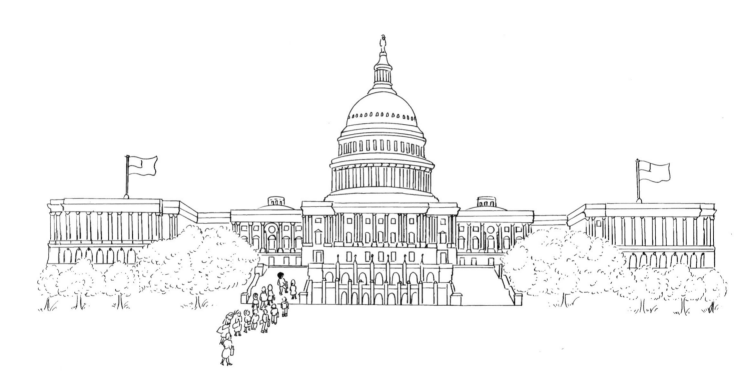

Capitol Hill

A Health Coalition was formed by five health systems agencies with the purpose of influencing legislation on health care issues in the U.S. Senate and the Congress. I was elected President of the Coalition for one term. In that capacity, I led a selected group of community leaders at least once a month to Capitol Hill to meet collectively with members of the U.S. Senate and the Congress. Then, we met the heavy-weight members individually to advance our causes. In addition, I directed campaigns on the local level.

HOME COMING

Since President Nixon's China visit, China opened up to the outside world. Between 1981 and 1983, I tried several times in New York City to secure a visa to see my family in China, but without success. I thought I might have a better chance to apply from Hong Kong, so I made a special trip for that purpose. Again, my request was rejected.

A family friend, whom I had never met, invited me to Macao with several of his friends. He gave me five thousand dollars for gambling in the biggest casino there.

Macao

I told him that I preferred to take a walk. I went down a quiet street a few thousand feet from the Casino. There was a very old man playing a two-stringed instrument, and a young, blind girl singing a very sad song. Hours later, on my way back, they were still there playing and singing. But the girl's voice had become hoarse, and the plate in front of them had only a few coins in it. A few blocks away, people were throwing hundreds, thousands, and millions of dollars onto the gambling tables, but here an old man and a young blind girl were struggling to beg for a few coins. The girl was like a flower that was withering before it had a chance to open, and the old man's life was almost spent. I wondered how long they could continue. It was a very tragic scene.

TRYING AGAIN

Family Reunion

Two years later, when I tried for a visa again, my application was approved. I was sent a long list of items my family needed and I first stopped in Hong Kong to purchase these gifts for them.

The next day I traveled by train to the city of Canton, First, I checked into a hotel and then went to visit my family.

My mother started sobbing. My sister reached out her hand to me but quickly withdrew it, half way. I guessed that when I was little, she must have often held my hand, but now, in front of her, I was no longer the little brother she used to know. I was glad to see them. However, I had been alone all those years. Family had become a strange thing to me. My father had passed away, and my adopted mother, the nun, was nowhere to be found.

I was also surrounded by many relatives that I had never known. My mother and her daughter-in-law had big problems. Every one of my family members wanted to talk to me about their plight in life. They all wanted me to take their side. Family matters were complicated.

I just listened and remained silent. My mother had a long talk with me. She told me of all the miseries and sufferings of her life. I suggested to her that the past had gone, and she should live for the future. I said, "The water of the Yangtze River brings millions of tons of water into the Pacific Ocean every moment. But the water we see at this moment is no longer the same water. It has already gone. Similarly, Whatever happened in the past no longer exists. It is a shadow in your mind. It is an illusion."

Strangely, nobody ever asked *me* how I had lived in those years of separation. It was an unusual family reunion. I found that our spiritual worlds were far apart. Then, after my mother passed away some years later, my connection with the family finally was severed. Yes, a falling leaf can never reattach to the tree. It only drifts, and drifts into the unknown.

DEMI

One rainy day, I met my future wife Demi when we ran into each other on a busy New York City street, each carrying an identical bright red lacquer Chinese umbrella with rainbow colored strings inside. We looked at each other and laughed. Quickly we two developed into a union.

Love is really a mysterious thing. It is the most beautiful music. The silent music. It fills every fiber of one's being.

Chinese International Conference

Demi is the creator of more than 150 illustrated books to date. The great, great granddaughter of the great painter William Morris Hunt. She was born with painting in her blood.

In the 80s, she was invited by New York City's Metropolitan Museum of Art to exhibit her work, which was very well received.

From then on, she has been invited by many organizations in the U.S. and other countries to give lectures and presentations of her work. I have been her partner in some of these activities.

She and I represented the United States at The First International Book Conference in Beijing, China in 1990. During that trip, I was very pleased to learn through personal contacts that many Chinese literati continued to carry the torch of the Chinese cultural tradition even after the massive destruction by the so-called "Cultural Revolution." China must not lose her soul.

The White House

Shortly after we returned to the U.S., we were invited by the former First Lady Barbara Bush to The White House for tea. Mrs. Bush's Cultural Incentive Program had selected one of Demi's books, "The Empty Pot" to be read on The ABC Radio Network Program called "Mrs. Bush's Story Time."

"The Empty Pot" has now developed into many forms, theatre, film, ballet and opera. We were invited to attend its first gala opera performance in London. During the celebration party after the performance, there was a discussion about music. Somebody suggested Beethoven was the greatest composer. Another mentioned Mozart. I said that Mozart was not a composer; that he was music himself. Beethoven and many other great composers had to work to compose, somewhat like squeezing milk from a cow. But for Mozart—music flowed out effortlessly like a fountain.

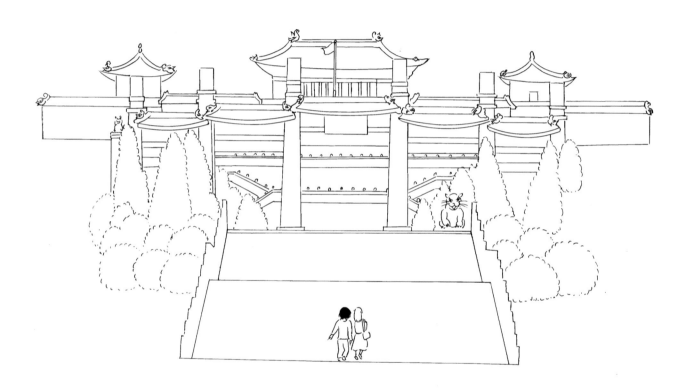

The Palace Museum in Taipei

My wife asked me to show her where I lived when I was in Taiwan. So we made a trip to visit the city of Taipei. The changes had been so dramatic that I could not even find my direction. The previous rice paddies had been transformed into block after block of high-rise buildings. Finally, we were able to find the hanging bridge that I used to walk across every day.

But the beautiful river below, where I once used to swim and play, was now so polluted that dead fish were floating on the surface.

One day we visited the Palace Museum. While we were appreciating the many paintings and treasures, a gentleman came up and asked me come to his Security Office. He said, "I am your former schoolmate. I am concerned about your safety here in Taiwan. I suggest that you leave the island as soon as possible, or you may face serious consequences." I did not know that man. But I heeded his advice. We cut short our trip and departed soon thereafter.

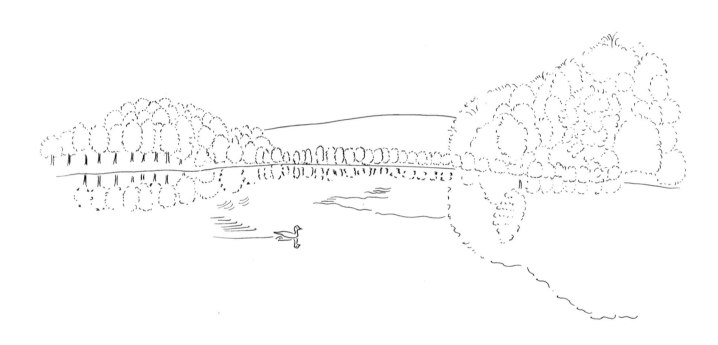

Remote Forest

We lived on Riverside Drive in Manhattan. Often we drove upstate, and walked in the remote forests and sat by the lakes, feeling the wind blowing through the trees, creating heavenly music. Looking at the reflected trees in the lake made me realize that the function of the human eye is also reflective.

No wonder so many people see things upside down and cause so much trouble in the world.

SEATTLE

After six years as Executive Director of the Health Systems Agency, it was time for me to move onto something else. I could not wait to devote myself to the spiritual pursuit. But, at that time, it was suggested that I take a senior position in the administration of the newly elected President of the United States. It was a highly political position.

Over the years I had observed that once a person is involved in politics, he is no longer a pussycat; he turns into a tiger, and I did not want to be in the field of tigers any more.

Cascade Mountains

We moved to Seattle to seek guidance from an Enlightened spiritual teacher. Shortly after we settled in the city of Bellevue, we experienced a series of black magic attacks and slander. I think demons are always ready to attack. They don't wait. But Buddha's time is Eternal. We had to be patient. To stay away from the hostile environment, we moved to a farm at the foot of the Cascade Mountains, and spent a few years working there and living in solitude.

The Richest Man's Party

Sometime later we returned to Bellevue.

In one of the richest American's home parties, we were guests on board his Emerald Star, cruising on Lake Washington. I sat with the president of a major U.S. company and his wife. We were discussing everything under the sun. At one point, his wife lamented the degradation of the American society.

She said that if people could follow Jesus' teaching to love your neighbor and love your enemy, the world would be more peaceful without so many wars. I commented, "But who is the neighbor and who is the enemy?

They are the same person. A stranger could not be your enemy because you are not related." Then I pointed to her husband and said jokingly,

"He is your enemy—but of course a good one." Then we all laughed.

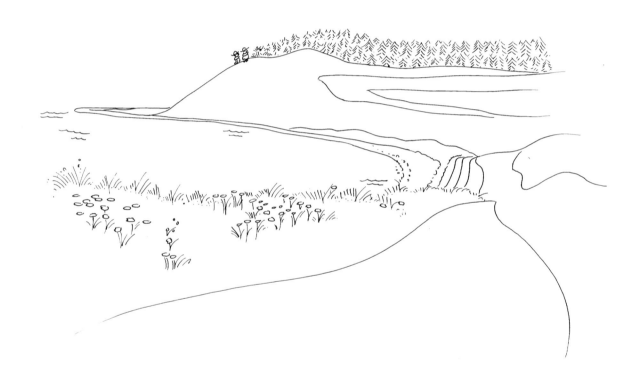

The Ocean and the Sky

After coming back to the city of Bellevue in recent years, we often take trips on the ferries to adjacent islands. We walk on the beaches of the Pacific Ocean. We sit on the high bluffs looking at the infinite vast sky. Then my heart becomes infinite and merges into one with the universe.

"What is life?" I was asked. There are almost seven billion people in the world today. So there are seven billion ways to look at life.

The Meaning of Life

The way I look at life is this: life is one thing that consists of two closely connected parts—the sum of one's desires, and the process to fulfill those desires. Desire is a bottomless pit. One desire fulfilled leads to many more desires. For most people, successes are few and failures are plenty.

Hence, pain and disappointments. There are things one wants to do but is not able to do, while at the same time there are things one does not want to do but has to do. Hence, frustrations. There are many choices one has to make. Each time one makes a choice, many other choices have to be given up. Hence regrets. At the end, one carries all the disappointments, frustrations, pain and regrets, and then leaves the world with great fear and agony.

But death is not the end of life. It is the opening to eternal liberation.

I am very fortunate that from a very young age I had the opportunity to taste many varieties and flavors of life. It has been challenging, difficult and painful. Yet, it has also been full of all the varieties, colors and music. Sometimes the color might have been gloomy or even dark and the music sad. Yet color and music are always beautiful a poetic. Yes, life is beautiful! Even the most desolate desert has its own beauty.

After years of practicing Buddha's teaching I have come to realize that *life* is the most precious gift that we have. For me, the meaning of life is that we transcend the mundane and reach the peak of self-realization, and then help others in their own self-realization.

I am very grateful to the many people who have helped me as well as to those who have hurt me. They are all my teachers. Indeed, every happening in my life has been my teacher.

Tze-si "Jesse" Huang is a professional writer and translator and native Chinese. He was born in Chungking, the youngest of ten children. After facing and overcoming trials of both survival and becoming educated, recorded in this book, he eventually immigrated to the U.S.A. He attended New York University and Columbia University for post graduate studies. In 1975, he met his wife, the renown children's book author and illustrator, Demi. In the United States he worked as a financial analyst and manager in several companies while continuing to pursue his love of writint and translating from his native Chinese into English. His award winning title *Master of Zen: Extraordinary Teachings from Hui Neng's Altar Sutra* is an example of his excellent work. In 1990, both Tze-si Huang and his wife, Demi, represented the United States at the First Children's International Book Conference in Beijing.

Demi is an award-winning illustrator of numerous books for children, including biographies of spiritual figures such as Jesus,. Muhammad, Buddha, the Dalai Lama, Saint Francis of Assisi, Lao Tzu, and Joan of Arc. Her books include *The Empty Pot, The Nightingale, The Emperor's New Clothes*, and *Gandhi*, which was named the *New York Times* Best Illustrated Book and received the Oppenheim Toy Portfolio Platinum Award.